# An Introduction to
# British
# Wild Flowers

## *A Photographic Guide*

Liz Gogerly

WAYLAND

This book is a differentiated text version of *The Wayland Book of Common British Wild Flowers* by Theresa Greenaway

First published in Great Britain in 2006 by Wayland, an imprint of Hachette Children's Books

Hachette Children's Books
338 Euston Road, London NW1 3BH

© Copyright 2006 Wayland

Editor: Camilla Lloyd
Senior Design Manager: Rosamund Saunders
Designer: Jane Hawkins

Archie Miles gratefully acknowledges the assistance of Cariann Clarke (flower diary), Freya Guest (seed planting) and the staff at Burley Gate C.E. Primary School.

Cover photograph: A wildflower meadow
Title page: Marsh marigolds growing in a pond.
This page (from top): Germander speedwell; bird's foot trefoil, meadow cranesbill; great burdock.
Contents page (from top): chickweed; common ragwort; field forget-me-not; red clover

### Picture credits

Eric Crichton 5 (middle & bottom)), 7 (top), 8 (bottom), 10 (all), 11 (bottom), 14 (bottom), 15 (all), 16 (middle), 17 (top), 18 (bottom), 19 (top), 20 (top), 21 (all), 22 (all), 23 (middle), 24 (middle & bottom), 25 (top), 26 (bottom), 27 (bottom), 28 (bottom), 29 (bottom), 31 (top), 33 (top & middle), 34 (all), 35 (all), 36 (bottom), 37 (bottom), 38 (top), 39 (all), 41 (top), 43 (inset), 45; Ecoscene Cover (Frank Blackburn) 40 (top), 43 (main); Hodder Wayland Picture Library 5 (top), 6 (top), 7 (bottom), 23 (top); Rowan McOnegal 14 (top), 29 (top & middle); Archie Milest title page, 4 (all), 6 (bulbous buttercups, middle, bottom), 8 (top), 9 (all), 11 (top), 12 (all), 13 (all), 14 (bottom right), 16 (top, bottom left & right), 17 (bottom), 18 (top), 19 (middle & bottom), 20 (middle & bottom), 23 (bottom), 25 (bottom), 26 (top), 27 (top & middle), 28 (top), 30 (top & middle), 31 (bottom), 32 (all), 33 (bottom), 36 (bluebells), 37 (top), 38 (bottom), 40 (bottom), 41 (bottom), 42, 44; Papilio 38 (bottom).

British Library Cataloguing in Publication Data

Gogerly, Liz
An introduction to British wild flowers
1. Wild flowers - Great Britain - Identification - Juvenile literature
I. Title
582.1'3'0941

ISBN-10: 0-7502-4990-0
ISBN-13: 978-0-7502-4990-4

Printed and bound in China

# Contents

# What are Wild Flowers?

There are thousands of different kinds of wild flowers. Many of them grow naturally in the countryside. They add to the beauty of the countryside but they are important in other ways too. Insects feed on the nectar produced by the flowers. Some mammals also eat wild flowers. Since ancient times wild flowers have been used to make herbal remedies.

## PARTS OF A WILD FLOWER

A wild flower plant is made up of roots, leaves, stems, and flowers. The flower contains the seeds of the plant. The roots fix the plant firmly into the soil and draw up water and nutrients from the soil. Each flower has sepals, petals, stamens and carpels. The sepals cover and protect the inner parts of the flower until it is ready to open. The petals attract insects with their colour and scent. Insects eat nectar, the sweet substance produced by the flower. The stamens are the male parts of the flower. The carpels are the female parts of the flower.

## PARTS OF A FLOWER

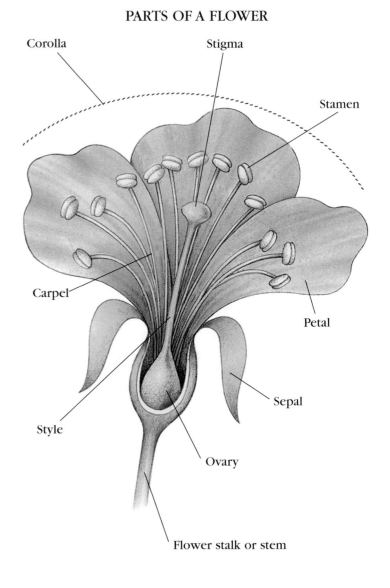

Corolla — Stigma — Stamen — Petal — Sepal — Ovary — Style — Carpel — Flower stalk or stem

▼ *Perforate St John's wort is a popular herbal remedy.*

▼ *The spots on the common spotted orchid attract insects.*

▼ *Insects feed on the sugary nectar from wild flowers.*

## FOOD

The leaves of wild flowers absorb energy from the sunlight. The energy is used to combine carbon dioxide from the air with water from the soil. This produces simple sugars. This process is called photosynthesis. The simple sugars, the nutrients, water from the soil and oxygen from the air allow the flower to grow.

## MAKING SEEDS

Wild flowers begin life as seeds. The seeds grow once pollen from the stamen reaches the carpel. The pollen is carried on the bodies of insects. When insects visit a flower, pollen sticks to their bodies. When these insects crawl over different flowers of the same kind the pollen clings to the stigma. The process is called pollination.

The pollen grains send tiny tubes down into the carpel. The tubes carry the male sex cells. These fuse with the female sex cells. This process is called fertilization. The seeds grow inside the carpel, which becomes the fruit of the plant. The fruit protects and feeds the growing seed.

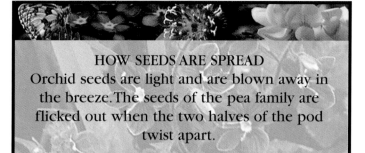

**HOW SEEDS ARE SPREAD**
Orchid seeds are light and are blown away in the breeze. The seeds of the pea family are flicked out when the two halves of the pod twist apart.

▶ *Pollen from the buttercup sticks to the body of this butterfly while it feeds on nectar.*

▼ *Each dandelion fruit is covered with fine hairs. These help to carry the seeds through the air.*

▼ *Great burdock seed heads have tiny hooks that attach to animals fur and are then spread over large distances.*

▼ *Blackberry seeds are spread by the animals that eat them.*

# Meadow buttercup

Scientific name: *Ranunculus acris*

Height: 30–100 cm

Family: buttercup

Flowering months: April–September

The meadow buttercup grows in meadows and gardens, along roadsides and in hedgerows. Like all buttercups it has no scent. Insects are attracted to the flower by its bright yellow petals. The leaves are hairy and rounded. Bulbous buttercups are similar to meadow buttercups. Meadow buttercups have sepals around the petals. Bulbous buttercups have sepals bent back from the petals.

▲ *A butterfly drinks nectar from a buttercup.*

◄ *Buttercups are one of Britain's most common wild flowers.*

# Creeping buttercup

Scientific name: *Ranunculus repens*

Height: 10–60 cm

Family: buttercup

Flowering months: May–August

▶ *The creeping buttercup soon covers an area with runners and new plants.*

The creeping buttercup spreads itself with its thick stems, called runners. The runners grow out sideways from the base of each plant. The roots and leaves of a new buttercup plant grow at the tip of each runner. The lower leaves of this plant are divided into three lobes. Each of the three lobes is divided into smaller lobes, with toothed edges.

# Marsh marigold

Scientific name: *Caltha palustris*

Height: 20–60 cm

Family: buttercup

Flowering months: March–July

▲ *The marsh marigold grows partly under water.*

The marsh marigold grows in damp places such as marshes or beside ponds and streams. It has heart-shaped, glossy, dark-green leaves with toothed edges. Its flowers have shiny yellow petals. They appear in spring and early summer.

▲ *Lesser celandine's flowers have 7–12 petals and three sepals.*

# Lesser celandine

| | |
|---|---|
| Scientific name: | *Ranunculus ficaria* |
| Height: | 5–25 cm |
| Family: | buttercup |
| Flowering months: | February–May |

Lesser celandine grows in damp soil, on sunny banks, and in woodlands and hedgerows. It is one of the first flowers to open each spring. It has yellow flowers from February onwards. The leaves are heart-shaped with smooth edges.

# Common poppy

| | |
|---|---|
| Scientific name: | Papaver rhoeas |
| Height: | 20–80 cm |
| Family: | poppy |
| Flowering months: | June–August |

The common poppy is also called the field poppy. It grows best on soil that has been broken up or disturbed like the soil that grain crops are grown on.

The common poppy has a branched stem. Its leaves are divided into narrow, toothed lobes. Each flower has four thin scarlet petals with a purple-black blotch at the base of the petal. The seeds grow in a seed capsule. The seeds can be shaken out when the capsule is ripe.

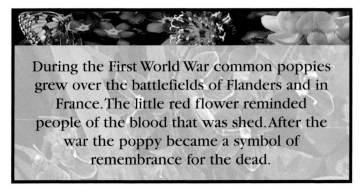

During the First World War common poppies grew over the battlefields of Flanders and in France. The little red flower reminded people of the blood that was shed. After the war the poppy became a symbol of remembrance for the dead.

▶ *The stems and leaves of the common poppy are covered with stiff hairs.*

# Shepherd's purse

| | |
|---|---|
| Scientific name: | *Capsella bursa-pastoris* |
| Height: | 3–40 cm |
| Family: | cress |
| Flowering months: | all year round |

The shepherd's purse is named after its heart-shaped fruits. It is a garden and farmland weed. It can grow in bare soil and in the cracks between paving stones.

At the base of each plant there is a ring of leaves that is arranged like a rosette. Flower stalks grow up from these leaves. These have smaller leaves and clusters of tiny white flowers at the top. When the petals fall off, heart-shaped fruits grow with seeds inside. Each fruit is on a stalk, which lengthens as the fruit ripens.

◀ *It is easy to recognise shepherd's purse by its heart-shaped fruits.*

# Garlic mustard

| | |
|---|---|
| Scientific name: | *Alliaria petiolata* |
| Height: | 20–120 cm |
| Family: | cress |
| Flowering months: | April–June |

Garlic mustard gets its name because when you crush its leaves they smell strongly of garlic. Garlic mustard is a tall, stiff plant. Its leaves are roughly heart-shaped, with a wavy or toothed edge. The caterpillar of the orange-tip butterfly particularly likes to eat the leaves.

At the top of the stem, there are small stalks. Each stalk bears white flowers. The flowers grow into long, narrow fruits. When the fruits ripen they split and release two rows of black seeds.

▶ *Garlic mustard is also known as Jack-by-the-hedge. It is common in hedgerows and roadsides.*

# Cuckoo flower

Scientific name: *Cardamine pratensis*

Height: 15–60 cm

Family: cress

Flowering months: April–June

Cuckoo flowers grow best in wet meadows or by streams. The cuckoo flower was given its name because it flowers when cuckoos arrive in Britain in spring. Its petals are lilac-coloured, pale or even white. Its leaves are divided into leaflets. The leaves growing in a rosette at the base of the plant are round, those on the stem are long and narrow.

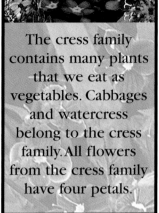

The cress family contains many plants that we eat as vegetables. Cabbages and watercress belong to the cress family. All flowers from the cress family have four petals.

◀ *Cuckoo flower is also called lady's smock.*

# Red campion

Red campion has sprays of pinkish-red flowers at the top of its tallest stems. Its fruits are oval capsules with tiny teeth at the tips. When the tips open the seeds are released. White campion and bladder campion look similar to red campion but they have white petals instead. The bladder campion has sepals that are joined together to make a papery 'bladder'.

Scientific name: *Silene dioica*

Height: 30–90 cm

Family: pink

Flowering months: May–June

◀ *Red campion flowers have five petals. Each flower measures about 18–25 mm wide.*

# Ragged robin

Scientific name: *Lychnis flos-cuculi*

Height: 30–75 cm

Family: pink

Flowering months: May–June

▶ *The ragged robin gets its name from its ragged petals.*

The ragged robin grows in damp meadows and marshes. It has narrow leaves with deep pink petals that are divided into four narrow lobes.

# Chickweed

**Scientific name:** *Stellaria media*

**Height:** 5–40 cm

**Family:** pink

**Flowering months:** all year round

▶ *Chickweed is similar to the greater stitchwort, the lesser stitchwort and the bog stitchwort.*

Chickweed is a common weed in gardens and farmland. It is a spreading plant with branched stems and oval, bright green leaves. Sprays of small, white flowers appear all year round. Flowers have five petals with deep notches at the tips. The green sepals are arranged like a star between each petal.

# Common dog violet

Common dog violet is one of the most common kinds of violet. It usually grows in grassy places, open woodland, hedgerows and pastures. It has heart-shaped leaves. Each flower has five mauve petals that grow singly on long stems. The lower petal has a slender, hollow shape. The seeds of the common dog violet grow in a capsule with three sections.

**Scientific name:** *Viola riviniana*

**Height:** 2–20 cm

**Family:** violet

**Flowering months:** April–June

◀ *Dog violets are from the same family as sweet violet, marsh violet and wild pansy.*

# Wood sorrel

Wood sorrel is a creeping plant. It spreads using underground stems. It prefers dry woodland, banks of hedges or shady rocks. The leaves and flowers of wood sorrel grow at the top of slender stems. Each leaf is divided into three heart-shaped leaflets. The white flowers have five petals with mauve-coloured veins.

**Scientific name:** *Oxalis acetosella*

**Height:** 5–15 cm

**Family:** wood sorrel

**Flowering months:** April–June

▲ *The leaves of wood sorrel hang downwards on the stem.*

# Perforate St John's wort

**Scientific name:** *Hypericum perforatum*

**Height:** 30–90 cm

**Family:** St John's wort

**Flowering months:** June–September

▶ *In the past people hung St John's wort in their homes. They believed it warded off evil spirits.*

Perforate St John's wort is most common on chalky soil. Look for its yellow flowers in grassy areas, open woodland or in banks of hedges.

Perforate St John's wort is a stiff upright plant with branched stems. Its leaves are oval and arranged opposite each other. Its leaves are covered in tiny dots.

Other members of the St John's wort family include slender St John's wort and square-stemmed St John's wort.

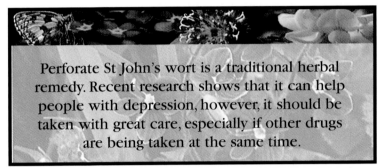

Perforate St John's wort is a traditional herbal remedy. Recent research shows that it can help people with depression, however, it should be taken with great care, especially if other drugs are being taken at the same time.

▲ *Bees love the nectar that the common mallow makes.*

# Common mallow

Common mallow is found in rough, grassy places. Look for it on roadsides and next to railway lines.

**Scientific name:** *Malva sylvestris*

**Height:** 45–90 cm

**Family:** mallow

**Flowering months:** June–September

The common mallow is a large plant with tough, branching stems. Its leaves are round in shape. Each leaf has 5-7 lobes with rounded, toothed edges. In the summertime the common mallow is filled with large pink flowers. These grow into fruits. The fruit is a ring of nutlets, each containing one seed.

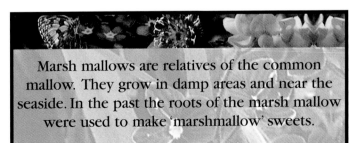

Marsh mallows are relatives of the common mallow. They grow in damp areas and near the seaside. In the past the roots of the marsh mallow were used to make 'marshmallow' sweets.

# Meadow cranesbill

The meadow cranesbill gets its name from the shape of its fruits. They have a part that sticks out like a beak or bill. The plant grows in clumps of leafy, branched stems. Its flowers have five violet-coloured petals. Its lower leaves are divided into lobes arranged like fingers of a hand.

Scientific name: *Geranium pratense*

Height: 30–80 cm

Family: geranium

Flowering months: June–September

▶ *Meadow cranesbill is widespread in meadows and on roadsides.*

# Herb robert

Scientific name: *Geranium robertianum*

Height: 10–50 cm

Family: geranium

Flowering months: May–September

◀ *Herb Robert will grow in woods, rocks, on shingle beaches and even on felled trees.*

Herb robert is a red-tinged plant with weak stems. Often it sprawls over other plants or rocks for support. The leaves are divided into leaflets. The leaflets are split into lobes which makes the leaves look like lace. Herb robert flowers are small and pink with five petals. Like the meadow cranesbill, herb robert has fruits with 'beaks'.

# Common bird's foot trefoil

Common bird's foot trefoil has stems that lie almost flat along the ground. It has pea-like yellow flowers. These are arranged in clusters of between two and seven flowers at the tops of upright stems. The flowers grow into seed pods that split when they are ripe.

Scientific name: *Lotus corniculatus*

Height: 10–40 cm

Family: pea

Flowering months: June–September

▶ *Common bird's foot trefoil grows in fields, heathlands and other grassy places.*

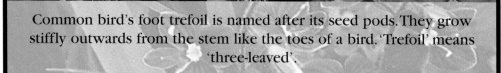

Common bird's foot trefoil is named after its seed pods. They grow stiffly outwards from the stem like the toes of a bird. 'Trefoil' means 'three-leaved'.

# White clover

| | |
|---|---|
| **Scientific name:** *Trifolium repens* | |
| **Height:** up to 30 cm | |
| **Family:** pea | |
| **Flowering months:** June–September | |

▶ *Bees are very fond of white clover and it is also known as 'bee bread'.*

White and red clover are common in fields, on the banks of hedges and other grassy places. White clover is a creeping plant. It has stems that can trail up to 50 centimetres long. It has clusters of white or pinkish flowers. Each leaf is divided into three leaflets with finely toothed edges. There is a mark in the shape of a 'V' in the centre of each leaf.

Red clover is similar to white clover. It has deep pink or reddish-purple flowers.

▶ *Red clover has a pair of leaves immediately below each flower head.*

# Tufted vetch

| | |
|---|---|
| **Scientific name:** *Vicia cracca* | |
| **Height:** 60–200 cm | |
| **Family:** pea | |
| **Flowering months:** June–August | |

There are a number of species of vetch. They are all climbing plants with long, weak stems. Vetches cling to the stems of stronger plants to support themselves. They can do this by coiling their tendrils around the stem of other plants.

Tufted vetch is one of the most widespread of the vetch family. It has spikes of bluish-purple flowers. Its leaves are divided into 6–15 pairs of narrow leaflets. Tendrils grow at the tip of each leaf.

▶ *The flowers of the tufted vetch grow into a seed pod containing six seeds.*

# Agrimony

Agrimony grows well in dry, grassy places. Look for it on roadsides, banks of hedges and chalk grasslands. It is a stiff upright plant with small yellow flowers.

**Scientific name:** *Agrimonia eupatoria*

**Height:** 30–60 cm

**Family:** rose

**Flowering months:** June–August

These grow into fruits covered in tiny hooks. These hooks cling to fur, feathers or clothing. The leaves of agrimony grow low down on the stem. These are divided into leaflets of different sizes.

◀ *The flowers of agrimony grow in clusters on a long stem.*

# Wild strawberry

**Scientific name:** *Fragaria vesca*

**Height:** 5–30 cm

**Family:** rose

**Flowering months:** April–July

▶ *Wild strawberries have a stronger flavour than cultivated strawberries.*

The wild strawberry grows in woodland and in hedge banks. It has long stems that arch over the ground. New plants grow at the tip of each stem. The leaves are divided into three toothed leaflets. Its white flowers grow into the little red fruits.

# Silverweed

Silverweed is common on dry, grassy places, wasteland, fields or roadsides. Silverweed gets its name from the silky, silvery hair that covers the underside of

**Scientific name:** *Potentilla anserina*

**Height:** 5–25 cm

**Family:** rose

**Flowering months:** May–August

each leaf. The leaves of the silverweed are divided into 7–12 pairs of toothed leaflets. It has single yellow flowers with five petals. It is a creeping plant with stems that can reach 80 centimetres long.

◀ *The yellow flowers of silverweed grow on leafless stems.*

# Dog rose

Scientific name: *Rosa canina*

Height: 1–3 metres

Family: rose

Flowering months: June–July

The dog rose is the most common wild rose growing in Britain's hedgerows. It has white or pink flowers that open in early summer.

The dog rose has arching woody stems covered in prickles. The prickles help the dog rose to cling to other shrubs and are sharp to touch. The flowers grow into hard woody nutlets. These are tightly packed inside a red, fleshy rounded fruit known as a 'rosehip'.

Burnet rose is similar to the dog rose. It is mostly found near the sea. Its creamy white flowers turn into purplish-black fruits.

▲ *The dog rose is very attractive to insects.*

The rosehip contains fibres that irritate human and animal skin. In the past, rosehips were used to making itching powder.

# Bramble

Scientific name: *Rubus fruticosus*

Height: Over 2 metres

Family: rose

Flowering months: May–September

The bramble is famous for its tasty blackberries and its sharp prickles. Its stems grow flat on the ground or grow over other shrubs and trees. The pink flowers of the bramble open from mid-summer onwards. All kinds of insects visit the flowers to collect nectar and pollen. Blackberries appear from August to October and the early fruits are usually the best.

▲ *Blackberries turn from green to yellow, then red to black. They are ready to eat when they are black.*

Ripe blackberries are a treat for birds and insects. Many people brave the prickles to go blackberry picking. They use the blackberries to make jams, puddings and wine.

# Meadowsweet

◀ *Meadowsweet flowers grow in sprays on branchlets.*

**Scientific name:** *Filipendula ulmaria*

**Height:** 60–120 cm

**Family:** rose

**Flowering months:** June–September

Meadowsweet grows in clumps near ponds and rivers. Its tiny white flowers have a strong, pleasant scent. Meadowsweet leaves are divided into leaflets with uneven toothed edges.

# Purple loosestrife

▲ *Purple loosestrife spreads quickly when it grows next to water.*

Purple loosestrife grows well besides water. It is a stiff-stemmed plant and looks greyish-green. The leaves are lance-shaped and grow all the way up the stem. It has spikes of reddish-purple flowers.

**Scientific name:**

*Lythrum salicaria*

**Height:** 60–120 cm

**Family:** loosestrife

**Flowering months:**

June–August

# Rosebay willowherb

Rosebay willowherb has become more common in the last 100 years. It grows well on dry patches of wasteland. After the Second World War it was widespread on bombed sites.

Rosebay willowherb has tall, straight stems. The leaves are lance-shaped. Its pinkish-purple flowers are out all summer long. They grow in a loose spike at the top of each stem. The fruit is a slender capsule. It splits to release fluffy seeds that are carried by the air.

▶ *Rosebay willowherb also spreads by using creeping underground stems.*

**Scientific name:** *Chamerion angustifolium*

**Height:** 30–120 cm

**Family:** willowherb

**Flowering months:** June–September

▶ *Flowers of the rosebay willowherb have four petals. The upper pair of petals are wider than the lower petals.*

# Cow parsley

Scientific name: *Anthriscus sylvestris*

Height: 60–100 cm

Family: carrot

Flowering months: April–June

Cow parsley grows along hedgerows and beside fields. It has flat heads of tiny white flowers. These grow in clusters at the end of slender stems. The stems are arranged like the spokes of an umbrella. Botanists call this type of flower head an umbel. This word comes from the Latin word *umbrella*, which means 'sunshade'.

Cow parsley belongs to the carrot family. Parts of some carrot family plants can be eaten but other members of the family are poisonous like cow parsley and should never be eaten.

▲ *Carrots, parsnips, fennel and parsley all belong to the same family. The leaves of cow parsley are divided three times into small leaflets.*

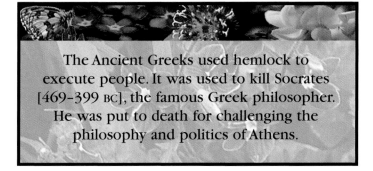

The Ancient Greeks used hemlock to execute people. It was used to kill Socrates [469–399 BC], the famous Greek philosopher. He was put to death for challenging the philosophy and politics of Athens.

# Hemlock

Scientfic name: *Conium maculatum*

Height: up to 2 metres

Family: carrot

Flowering months: June–July

Hemlock grows best in damp soil. Look for it on patches of wasteland, beside ditches and roadsides. Hemlock is a member of the carrot family. It is very poisonous and can even kill. It looks similar to cow parsley because it has clusters of white flowers on slender stems. The stems are also arranged like the spokes of an umbrella. However, the leaves of hemlock look lacier than leaves of cow parsley. Hemlock also has purple spots on its tall stems.

Another harmful member of the carrot family is Giant hogweed. If you touch this plant you can get painful blisters.

◄ *Hemlock is poisonous. Other members of the carrot family that are harmful include fool's parsley, hemlock water dropwart and cowbane.*

# Goosegrass

**Scientific name:** *Galium aparine*

**Height:** 15–120 cm

**Family:** bedstraw

**Flowering months:** May–September

▶ *Goosegrass leaves are arranged in whorls of 6–8 along the stem.*

Goosegrass grows well in hedges and is a common weed on farms. Goosegrass is also known as cleavers because it clings to clothes with its prickles. The prickles grow along the plant's square stems and the edges of its leaves. Goosegrass has weak stems. The prickles help the plant to grow over other plants or walls for support.

Goosegrass has clusters of tiny white flowers. Its fruit has two rounded lobes that are covered with tiny hooked bristles. Like the stems and the leaves, the fruits attach themselves to fur, feathers and clothing.

# Teasel

**Scientific name:** *Dipsacus fullonum*

**Height:** 50–200 cm

**Family:** teasel

**Flowering months:** July–August

The teasel can be very prickly to touch. It has prickles growing along it stiff square stem. There are also sturdy, hooked prickles growing underneath its leaves. The leaves are arranged in pairs up the stem. At the base of the plant the leaves are joined together. They form a cup in which rainwater can collect for the plant.

The flower head of the teasel is made up of a mass of tiny, lilac-coloured flowers. Each flower is enclosed in a bristly cup. In late summer some birds like to peck the seeds out of the flower heads.

◀ *In the past wool spinners and cloth makers used the hooked bristle collected from a special variety of teasel.*

# Biting stonecrop

**Scientific name:** *Sedum acre*

**Height:** 2–10 cm

**Family:** stonecrop

**Flowering months:** May–July

Biting Stonecrop can grow in very dry places. It appears on rocks and walls, and in waste ground, dry grassland and sand dunes. It survives by storing water in its thick fleshy leaves. Biting stonecrop is sometimes known as wall pepper. It has creeping stems that spread out to make a mat. It has masses of bright yellow flowers.

▲ *Biting stonecrop has star-shaped flowers. There are so many flowers that often its leaves are completely hidden.*

# Harebell

▲ *The bell-shape protects the pollen from the rain.*

Harebell grows on dry, chalky grassland. It has slender, upright stems. The leaves that grow at its base are almost round. The leaves on the stem are long and narrow.

**Scientific name:** *Campanula rotundifolia*

**Height:** 15–50 cm

**Family:** bellflower

**Flowering months:** July–September

Harebell has delicate lilac flowers. The flowers are bell-shaped which is where it gets its name. Seeds grow inside a rounded capsule. When the seeds are ripe they are released through tiny holes. The seeds are dispersed as the flower moves in the breeze.

# Heather

**Scientific name:** *Calluna vulgaris*

**Height:** up to 60 cm

**Family:** heather

**Flowering months:** July–September

▶ *Heather has small leaves. These grow close to the stem and look like scales.*

Heather often covers large areas of heathland or spreads over hillsides. It is made up of lots of tiny rose-purple flowers. When they are in bloom the whole area looks beautiful. Heather is a small woody shrub. It has many thin, branched stems. These grow upright or sprawl over the ground.

# Daisy

Scientific name: *Bellis perennis*

Height: 4–12 cm

Family: daisy

Flowering months: March–October

▶ *Daisies grow well on the short turf of lawns. Many gardeners treat them like weeds.*

Daisies were named after the Old English words for 'day's eye' because the flowers close at night and open in the day. Each daisy head has two kinds of flower or floret. Those at the centre of the daisy head are yellow and tubular. Surrounding these are florets with white petals.

▲ *Ox-eye daisies grow well in meadows and hedgerows. They prefer chalky or fertile soil.*

# Ox-eye daisy

The ox-eye daisy is bigger than the daisy. It has lobed leaves growing up its stems (the daisy only has leaves growing at its base). The ox-eye daisy has oval leaves growing at its base. Its flower head is like the daisy because it is made of two kinds of florets.

Scientific name: *Leucanthemum vulgare*

Height: 20–70 cm

Family: daisy

Flowering months: June–August

# Yarrow

Scientific name: *Achillea millefolium*

Height: 8–60 cm

Family: daisy

Flowering months: June–August

▶ *Yarrow is a common garden plant.*

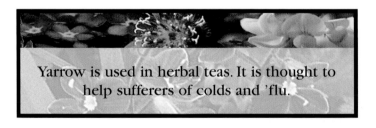

Yarrow is used in herbal teas. It is thought to help sufferers of colds and 'flu.

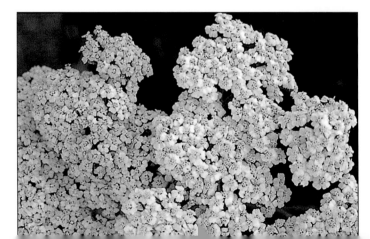

Yarrow grows well in grassy places such as meadows, gardens and hedgerows. It has striking, pure white, pinkish-white or pinkish flowers. It has long green leaves divided into tiny narrow leaflets. These feathery leaves have a pleasant fragrance when they are crushed.

# Common ragwort

**Scientific name:** *Senecio jacobaea*

**Height:** 30–150 cm

**Family:** daisy

**Flowering months:** June–October

Common ragwort is a sturdy plant that grows quickly. Look for it growing on pastures, roadsides and wastelands. Striking daisy-like yellow flowers grow on the top of its branched stems. It has a rosette of leaves growing at the base of the plant. It also has narrow leaves growing up its stems. The seeds are found inside tough fruits. Each fruit has cottony hair which help the seeds fly through the air.

Ragwort has an unpleasant fragrance when it is bruised. This is the plant's way of letting animals know that it is poisonous. It is especially dangerous to grazing animals such as cattle and horses.

▲ *Common ragwort is a pest to livestock farmers. It is difficult to destroy and spreads easily.*

Dandelion leaves can be eaten. They are used in salads or to make wine or tea.

▼ *The dandelion fruit is also called a dandelion 'clock'. Children love to blow the seeds away.*

# Dandelion

**Scientific name:** *Taraxacum officinale*

**Height:** 5–40 cm

**Family:** daisy

**Flowering months:** March–October

The dandelion is one of the most common wild flowers in Britain. It springs up almost everywhere! The word 'dandelion' comes from the French word dents de lion, which means 'lion's teeth'. It got this name because its long, lobed leaves look like large teeth. The dandelion flower head has ray florets surrounded with yellow petals. The flower head eventually becomes a round mass of small, single-seeded fruits. Each fruit has a crown of stiff white hairs. The hairs help the seeds blow away in the wind.

# Spear thistle

**Scientific name:** *Cirsium vulgare*

**Height:** 30–150 cm

**Family:** daisy

**Flowering months:** July–October

The spear thistle has sharp spines growing on its stems. There are also prickly spines growing on the green base of each flower head. These spines prevent animals from eating the plant. The spear thistle has flower heads arranged in dense clusters at the tip of each branch. Each flower head is roughly oval-shaped with pinkish-purple florets. The flower eventually turns into a fluffy seed ball. The seeds are then spread by the wind. The dwarf and marsh thistle are other very prickly kinds of thistles.

▶ *The spear thistle belongs to the daisy family.*

# Great burdock

**Scientific name:** *Arctium lappa*

**Height:** 90–130 cm

**Family:** daisy

**Flowering months:** July–September

Great burdock is found on wasteland, hedgerows and clearings. It is a sturdy, bushy plant. Its large leaves are heart-shaped with deep grooves. The flower heads of the great burdock are round. It has tiny purple florets but these are almost hidden inside a cup of scaly bracts. Each bract has a hook at the tip. These hooks attach themselves to passing animals. The whole fruit head is then carried away and the seeds are scattered.

◀ *The bracts of the great burdock often stick on to clothing when people go walking in the countryside.*

▲ *In spring primroses cover hedge banks and woodland clearings.*

# Primrose

Scientific name: *Primula vulgaris*

Height: 8–20 cm

Family: primrose

Flowering months: January-May

Primrose flowers are yellowish-white. A single flower grows on a slender stem. Each of the five petals has a deep notch at its tip. The flowers rise up from a dense clump of leaves. These leaves are roughly oblong-shaped with toothed edges. They are wrinkled and have hairs on the lower surface.

# Creeping jenny

Creeping jenny grows best in moist, slightly shaded, grassy places. The plant is only a few centimetres high but it spreads

Scientific name:
*Lysimachia nummularia*

Height: about 5 cm

Family: daisy

Flowering months: May–July

over great distances. Its trailing stems are up to 60 centimetres long. The flowers have five, slightly cupped, yellow petals. The lobes of the petals are sprinkled with black dots.

▲ *Pairs of round leaves grow along each stem.*

▲ *Flowers of the scarlet pimpernel like the sunshine. They open at about 8.00am and close at about 3.00pm. They shut when it rains.*

# Scarlet pimpernel

Scarlet pimpernel is a common weed. It is usually found in crop fields, gardens, roadsides or sand dunes. Its stems drape over the ground. It has roughly oval leaves. The lower surface of each leaf is

Scientific name:
*Anagallis arvensis*

Height: 5–20 cm

Family: daisy

Flowering months:
May–October

speckled with black dots. Its small red flowers have five petals. Seeds grow inside a small round capsule.

# Field forget-me-not

**Scientific name:** *Myosotis arvensis*

**Height:** 15–30 cm

**Family:** borage

**Flowering months:** April–September

▶ *The flowers of the field forget-me-nots are at their best in May.*

Common forget-me-not is also called field forget-me-not. It grows best in dry, sunny places. Some people plant forget-me-nots in their gardens for the blanket of colour they bring. Other people think of it as a weed.

The flowers of the forget-me-not are pale blue with yellow centres. Although the flowers are small, they grow in dainty clusters. The leaves and stems are slightly hairy.

Forget-me-nots have always been a symbol of lasting love and friendship. A sprig of forget-me-not in a wedding bouquet is a symbol of true love.

# Viper's bugloss

Viper's bugloss is also known as blue thistle. It is a stiff, upright plant with prickly hairs on its stems. The leaves are long and narrow. Its flowers are arranged in sprays up the stem. They are reddish before changing to a deep purple colour.

**Scientific name:** *Echium vulgare*

**Height:** 30–90 cm

**Family:** borage

**Flowering months:** June–September

▲ *Each flower has stamens that are longer than the petals.*

# Common comfrey

**Scientific name:** *Symphytum officinale*

**Height:** 30–120 cm

**Family:** borage

**Flowering months:** May–July

▶ *Common comfrey leaves feels rough to touch.*

Common comfrey grows in damp places, often beside streams, rivers and ponds. It is a large plant. Its stems and leaves are covered in bristly hairs. The leaves are roughly oval in shape. It has sprays of tubular flowers. These can be creamy white, pink or purple.

# Field bindweed

**Scientific name:** *Convolvulus arvensis*

**Height:** 20–75 cm

**Family:** convolvulus

**Flowering months:** June–September

Field bindweed grows well in light, dry soil that has been broken up. This is why it is common on farmland. Farmers find it a pest and cannot get rid of it very easily. This is because its roots can grow over 2 metres into the ground.

Field bindweed has long, weak stems. The plant creeps over the ground and twists itself around other plants for support. It has pale, funnel-shaped flowers. The leaves are oval or arrow-shaped.

▲ *The flowers of the field bindweed can be white, pink or pink and white.*

# Hedge bindweed

**Scientific name:** *Calystegia sepium*

**Height:** up to 3 metres

**Family:** convolvulus

**Flowering months:** July–September

Hedge bindweed grows well on railway embankments, farmland and waste ground. It is also a common weed in gardens.

Hedge bindweed has sturdier stems than field bindweed. It can climb up hedges with its twining stems. Often it will cover a whole bush or fence. It has large attractive flowers. The leaves are big and arrow-shaped. Its seeds grow in small capsules that split to release the seeds.

Gardeners do not like it because it smothers other plants. It spreads rapidly using creeping underground stems.

◀ *The flowers of the hedge bindweed close at night and open at dawn.*

# Bittersweet

**Scientific name:** *Solanum dulcamara*

**Height:** 30–200 cm     **Family:** potato

**Flowering months:** June–September

Bittersweet belongs to the potato family. This family has many poisonous plants. All parts of bittersweet are dangerous to eat and can cause death. Another member of the potato family is deadly nightshade. Just five small berries from this plant can kill a child.

▲ *In the centre of each bittersweet flower, the stamens join together to make a yellow 'cone'.*

Bittersweet is also known as woody nightshade. It is a climbing plant that grows in hedgerows, wasteland and on shingle beaches. It has oval-shaped leaves and heart-shaped leaves. The flowers are purple to pale blue. In late summer bittersweet produces bright red berries.

# Foxglove

The foxglove is easily recognizable by its bell-shaped purple flowers. They look a little

**Scientific name:** *Digitalis purpurea*

**Height:** 50–150 cm

**Family:** figwort

**Flowering months:** June–September

like the fingers of a glove. Each flower has a lower lip, and inside there are dark spots. In summer you will often see insects crawling inside the flower to reach the nectar. Foxglove leaves are oval-shaped. They are greyish-green, hairy and look wrinkled.

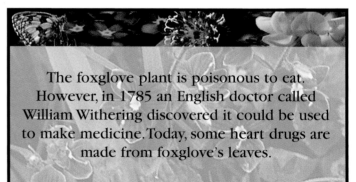

The foxglove plant is poisonous to eat. However, in 1785 an English doctor called William Withering discovered it could be used to make medicine. Today, some heart drugs are made from foxglove's leaves.

◀ *Foxglove flowers grow up one side of a tall, stiff stem.*

# Great mullein

Scientific name: *Verbascum thapsus*

Height: 30–200 cm

Family: figwort

Flowering months: June–September

▶ *Great mullein grows besides roads and in dry stony places.*

Great mullein has yellow, bell-shaped flowers. These grow on tall, sturdy stems. It has lance-shaped leaves. The leaves, stems and flower buds of the great mullein are covered in soft white hairs. This makes the plant appear pale green and very soft to touch.

▲ *Wasps are attracted to the nectar of the common figwort.*

◀ *Common figwort has branched, square stems.*

# Common figwort

Scientific name: *Scrophularia nodosa*

Height: 40–80 cm

Family: figwort

Flowering months: June–September

Common figwort grows in damp places in woodland clearings, hedgerows and beside water. It has roughly oval-shaped leaves. The edges of the leaves are unevenly toothed. Common figwort has small purplish-brown flowers. These are arranged in a loosely branched flower head at the top of each stem. They are pollinated by wasps.

# Ivy-leaved toadflax

Scientific name: *Cymbalaria muralis*

Stem length: 10–80 cm

Family: figwort

Flowering months: May–September

▶ *Its leaves and stems have a purple tinge.*

Ivy-leaved toadflax has creeping stems that spread over the ground or hang down over rocks and walls. It has tiny violet flowers with a patch of yellow on the lower petal. The leaves are kidney-shaped with five lobes.

# Germander speedwell

Scientific name: *Veronica chamaedrys*

Height: 20–40 cm

Family: figwort

Flowering months: March–July

Germander speedwell grows well in woodlands and grassy areas, hedges and on embankments. It has clusters of bright-blue flowers. The leaves are hairy and almost triangular-shaped. It has small, heart-shaped seed capsules. Germander speedwell is a relative of a weed called common field speedwell.

▶ *Germander speedwell flowers have four blue petals with a white centre.*

# White deadnettle

Scientific name: *Lamium album*

Height: 20–60 cm

Family: mint

Flowering month: April–November

White deadnettle has leaves that look similar to the stinging nettle (see page 31) but they don't have any of the sting. It has heart-shaped coarsely toothed leaves that are covered in fine hair. The creamy white flowers are tube-shaped and end in lobes. They grow in whorls around the stem.

White deadnettle belongs to the mint family. Like other members of this family it has square stems. Red deadnettle is similar to white deadnettle. It has purplish-pink flowers and the upper leaves have a reddish purple tinge.

◀ *White deadnettle grows almost anywhere but prefers to be in the sun.*

# Self-heal

Scientific name: *Prunella vulgaris*

Height: 5–30 cm   Family: mint

Flowering months: June–November

▶ *Self-heal has tubular, lipped, purple flowers.*

Self-heal covers gardens or playing fields like a mat. It grows so close to the ground that it isn't even cut by lawnmowers. When it is left to grow in woodland and grassy areas it can grow quite tall. Self-heal has oval-shaped leaves with shallow teeth around the edges.

The leaves, stems and flower heads of self-heal were once used to heal wounds.

# Skullcap

◀ *The flowers of the skullcap are tiny compared to its bushy leaves.*

Scientific name: *Scutellaria galericulata*

Height: 15–50 cm

Family: mint

Flowering months: June–September

Skullcap often grows next to streams or other damp, grassy places. It has a mass of lance-shaped leaves. Its violet-blue flowers are arranged in pairs up the stem. They are slender and tube-shaped. Lesser skullcap is similar but it is smaller with pink flowers.

# Wood sage

Scientific name: *Teucrium scorodonia*

Height: 15–30 cm   Family: mint

Flowering months: July–September

Wood sage grows well in sandy heathlands, dry grasslands and woods. It grows in clumps of upright, woody stems. The leaves are heart-shaped, hairy and wrinkled. The pale green flowers are narrow and tube-shaped. They have a long lower lip that bends backwards. Two maroon pollen sacs stick out from the top of each flower.

▲ *Wood sage flowers are arranged along one side of the stem.*

# Greater plantain

The greater plantain is also known as the common plantain. It grows well in open, grassy places, crop fields and on roadsides. The large, oval leaves of the greater plantain are arranged in a rosette at the base of the plant. Its spikes of small flowers grow on tall stems. The white petals are tiny. The greater plantain spreads easily using wind pollination.

Scientific name: *Plantago major*

Height: 10–35 cm

Family: plantain

Flowering months: June–October

◄ *The stamens of the greater plantain are long and stick out from the flowers.*

# Curled dock

Curled dock is a weed commonly found on farmland. It has stiff upright stems. The large, lance-shaped leaves have wavy edges. Its small flowers are greenish in colour.

Scientific name: *Rumex crispus*

Height: 50–100 cm

Family: dock

Flowering months: June–October

► *Curled dock's tiny flowers are arranged in dense, closely-packed whorls.*

# Sun spurge

◄ *Sun spurge is poisonous. When the stem is cut it oozes a milky white sap that irritates human and animal skin.*

Scientific name:
*Euphorbia helioscopa*

Height: 10–50 cm

Family: spurge

Flowering months: May–August

Sun spurge is widespread on farmland or soil that has been disturbed. It has tall, unbranched stems. Spoon-shaped leaves grow all the way up the stem. The leaves are broadest towards the tip and narrower at the stem. From May onwards it has yellow flowers. These are surrounded by whorls of green bracts that look like leaves.

# Stinging nettle

**Scientific name:** *Urtica dioica*

**Height:** 30–150 cm    **Family:** nettle

**Flowering months:** June–September

▶ *The scientific name for stinging nettles is 'urtica dioica'. This come from the Latin word 'uro' which means 'I burn'.*

Stinging nettles are well known because they sting when you touch them. The 'sting' tingles and irritates the skin for up to a day. They are usually found in rich, fertile soil on farmland or neglected gardens.

Stinging nettles grow in large patches of stiff, upright stems. The heart-shaped leaves are arranged in opposite pairs up the stem. They are dark green with coarsely toothed edges. The leaves and stems of the stinging nettle are covered in sharp stinging hairs. The stinging nettle has male and female flowers which grow on separate plants. The male flowers grow as long catkins. Female flowers grow in tighter clusters.

Stinging nettles lose their sting when they are cooked. They are nutritious and full of vitamins and minerals.

# Mistletoe

Mistletoe grows on the branches of trees such as apple, lime, poplar and hawthorn. Botanists call mistletoe a semi-parasite. This is because it makes its own food

**Scientific name:** *Viscum album*

**Height:** up to 1 metre

**Family:** mistletoe

**Flowering months:** February–April.

by photosynthesis. However, it takes the water and nutrients it needs from the tree on which it is growing.

Mistletoe has yellowish-green stems and leaves. Each stem branches out many times. This means the plant can grow up to 2 metres across. The separate male and female flowers are small and green. These grow into white berries.

◀ *It is easier to spot mistletoe in winter when the trees have lost their leaves.*

In ancient times people believed that mistletoe improved a woman's fertility. This could be where the custom of kissing under the mistletoe came from.

# Himalayan balsam

**Scientific name:** *Impatiens glandulifera*

**Height:** 1–2 metres

**Family:** balsam

**Flowering months:** July–October

▶ *The Himalayan balsam is also known as 'policeman's helmet'. This is because it is shaped like a British policeman's helmet.*

Himalayan balsam was brought to Britain in 1839. It was planted in gardens but it soon spread to the wild. These days it is most common next to streams and rivers. It grows fast and is a pest because it casts shade over smaller plants.

The Himalyan balsam has thick, fleshy stems. It has oval, toothed leaves that usually grow in opposite pairs or whorls of three. The flowers are arranged in sprays. They can be pink, purplish or white. The ripe seed capsule explodes when it is touched. This causes the seeds to shoot out in all directions.

# Common spotted orchid

▼ *Many orchids are rare but the common spotted orchid is widespread.*

**Scientific name:** *Dactylorhiza fuchsii*

**Height:** 25–50 cm  **Family:** orchid

**Flowering months:** June–August

The common spotted orchid is widespread throughout most of Britain. It grows in all kinds of places including woods, hedgerows, roadsides and meadows.

This striking plant has tall stems. Its narrow leaves are blotched with dark spots. The flowers are tube-shaped with a short spur pointing backwards. At the front of the tube there are two pink wing-shaped sepals and a three-lobed lip. The lip of each flower is patterned with lines and dots. The petals are in various shades of white and pink.

The common spotted orchid is a relative of the vanilla orchid that grows in tropical climates. It is used to produce vanilla flavouring.

# Common twayblade

Common twayblade is widespread in chalky soils on woodlands, moorlands and damp hedgerows. Each plant has just one pair of leaves. These oval leaves have 3–5 ribs. The greenish flowers grow on a thin spike.

Scientific name: *Listera ovata*

Height: 20–60 cm

Family: orchid

Flowering months: May–July

◀ *Each tiny green flower has a 'hood' of sepals and petals. It has a long lip that is deeply notched.*

# Yellow flag

Scientific name: *Iris pseudacorus*

Height: 40–150 cm

Family: Iris

Flowering months: June–August

▶ *Yellow flag flowers change into seed capsules. These cylinder-shaped capsules contain reddish-brown seeds.*

Yellow flag grows in patches beside water. It has tall, sword-shaped leaves. These grow from a thick, creeping stem. The leaves are bluish-green with a mid-rib. Each flower stem has 2–3 large yellow flowers. The structure of the flowers is quite complicated. Three floral parts are broad and curve downwards. The three other floral parts are smaller, narrower and curve upwards.

# Ramsons

Scientific name: *Allium ursinum*

Height: 25–45 cm

Family: lily

Flowering months: April–June

▶ *After the rain, the garlicky smell from ramsons fills the air.*

Ramsons often grow in large clumps in damp woodland, hedges or shaded corners in wet meadows. Ramsons is also known as wild garlic. Its bright green leaves smell strongly of garlic. Its upright stem has three sides. Each rounded flower head has about 6–20 flowers. The flowers have white petals and sepals. They look particularly striking when they are in full bloom.

# Water plants

Certain wild flowers only grow in water or on extremely damp ground. Some of these plants have all their leaves underwater. Others have leaves that float on the surface. The pond water crowfoot has underwater and floating leaves. Other water plants grow with just their roots permanently covered in water.

Water plants often have water-storing stems. Nutrients and gases such as carbon dioxide and oxygen are absorbed through the stems and roots. Water plants also have many air spaces in their stems and leaves. These help to keep the leaves afloat. When water plants are out of water they wilt and quickly dry out.

# White water lily

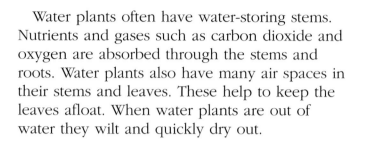

◀ *White water leaves are round with a deep split where the leaf joins the stem.*

| | |
|---|---|
| **Scientific name:** *Nymphaea alba* | |
| **Stem length:** up to 3 metres | |
| **Family:** water lily | |
| **Flowering months:** June–September | |

The white water lily has large flowers that measure 10–20 centimetres wide. Each flower has 20–25 white petals and a mass of yellow stamens in the centre. White water lily leaves are thick and almost circular in shape.

# Bogbean

| |
|---|
| **Scientific name:** *Menyanthes trifoliata* |
| **Stem length:** 10–35 cm |
| **Family:** bogbean |
| **Flowering months:** April–June |

▶ *Bogbean leaves are divided into three oval leaflets.*

Bogbean grows best in shallow water at the edge of ponds, lakes and rivers. It also grows in the wetter parts of marshes and bogs.

The leaves and flower heads grow well above the surface of the water. The flowers are white flushed with pink. Its petals are fringed.

# Bulrush

**Scientific name:** *Typha latifolia*

**Height:** 1.5–3 metres

**Family:** reed mace

**Flowering months:** July–August

Bulrush grows at the edges of ponds, lakes and slow-flowing rivers. It has sword-shaped leaves that stand stiffly upright. At the top of each plant there are tiny, yellow male flowers arranged in a spike. Below these flowers are tiny, reddish-brown female flowers. These are clustered tightly together to make a thick brown cylinder that is fuzzy to the touch. In the spring the 'cylinder' splits open and releases hundreds of fluffy seeds.

◀ *Another name for bulrush is reed-mace. Its reddish-brown flowers are easy to identify.*

# Common duckweed

**Scientific name:** *Lemna minor*

**Frond:** 1.5–4 mm wide

**Family:** duckweed

**Flowering months:** June-July

Duckweed plants spread quickly over garden ponds, canals and still water. A tiny duckweed plant does not have leaves. It just has rounded, green, pad-like 'fronds'. These float on the surface of the water. Each frond has one thin root that dangles down into the water. Common duckweed hardly ever flowers.

▶ *In this photograph you can see the pale green fronds of common duckweed. The dark red fronds are of the Azolla fern.*

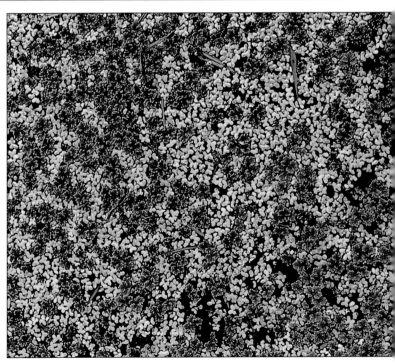

# Woodland flowers

Woodlands provide shelter and rich fertile soil for plants. They also have tall trees that cast deep shade on the ground below where their leaves are. Woodland flowers have adapted to these conditions. Plants need light to grow. Many woodland flowers open in spring before the leaves on the trees are out. This way, they make enough food to store until the next spring and produce seeds. When summer arrives, the leaves of these plants have already died. There is no sign of them except the ripening fruits. Other woodland flowers get enough light by climbing up taller plants. Honeysuckle climbs using long, arching stems that twist around other plants. Ivy climbs using tiny root-like suckers that cling to other plants.

▶ *Each bluebell flower is just like a bell hanging from a central flower stem.*

▼ *Bluebell flowers have a lovely sweet scent.*

## Bluebell

| | |
|---|---|
| **Scientific name:** *Hyacinthoides non-scripta* | |
| **Height:** 20–50 cm | **Family:** lily |
| **Flowering months:** April–June | |

Bluebells are in full flower in May. At this time woodlands are covered in masses of bluebells. Many people go out into the woods just to see this beautiful sight. Bluebell leaves are narrow and glossy green. The flowers are drooping blue 'bells' arranged in curved sprays. Bluebell seeds are black and grow in a capsule.

## Ground ivy

| | |
|---|---|
| **Scientific name:** *Glechoma hederacea* | |
| **Height:** 10–25 cm | |
| **Family:** mint | |
| **Flowering months:** March–September | |

▶ *Leaves and stems have an aromatic smell when crushed.*

Ground ivy creeps over the ground of woodland glades. It has square stems and kidney-shaped leaves. The leaves and stems are covered with soft hairs. They are often tinged with purple. The purple flowers are arranged in clusters, all facing in the same direction. Each flower has a tube-shaped base, with spots on the lower lip.

# Honeysuckle

**Scientific name:** *Lonicera periclymenum*

**Height:** up to 6 metres          **Family:** honeysuckle

**Flowering months:** June–October

Honeysuckle is well known for its sweet, strong smell. This is strongest in the evening and attracts all kinds of insects. Honeysuckle has oval, bluish green leaves. The flowers grow in clusters at the tips of short stems. Each flower has a long tube-shaped 'throat', with curled upper and lower lips. The stamen and upper part of the carpel stick out from the flower. Insects brush against the stamen when they gather nectar at the base of the tube.

▲ *Honeysuckle has bright, shiny berries that are a tasty treat for birds.*

◀ *Honeysuckle attracts insects such as hawkmoths.*

# Wood anemone

**Scientific name:** *Anemone nemorosa*

**Height:** 6–30 cm          **Family:** buttercup

**Flowering months:** March–May

Wood anemones can carpet large areas of the woodland floor. Their delicate, deeply-lobed leaves appear in late February onwards. The white or pinkish-white flowers open from March to May. The flowers only open when the sun shines on them. As soon as the leaves grow on the trees around them the flowers disappear. Only the roots remain until the next spring.

▶ *Each wood anemone flower has six petals.*

# Seaside flowers

Behind most beaches there is a strip of sand, shingle or rocks where the sea rarely reaches. It is difficult for plants to grow in these places. There is plenty of light but there is no shelter from harsh weather. Also, rain water quickly drains away.

Most seaside plants have special characteristics to help them to survive.

Seaside wild flowers have long roots that reach deep into the ground for water. These roots bind the sand or shingle and stop it from being blown away. Seaside wild flowers often have thick waxy or fleshy leaves. These leaves are used to store water. They are also tough so they are not damaged by the strong winds that sweep along coastal areas.

▲ *Sea sandwort is like a net. Shells and rubbish are caught in its stems.*

## Sea sandwort

Sea sandwort is one of the first plants to grow on freshly blown sand. It has creeping stems with many branches. These spread across the sand to form a mat. Sea sandwort has a large root system. These roots prevent the sand from blowing away.

| | |
|---|---|
| **Scientific name:** *Honkenya peploides* | |
| **Height:** 5–25 cm | |
| **Family:** pink | |
| **Flowering months:** May–August | |

Sea sandwort has thick, oval-shaped leaves. They are arranged opposite each other along the stems. The greenish-white flowers can be male or female.

# Yellow-horned poppy

| |
|---|
| **Scientific name:** *Glaucium maritimum* |
| **Height:** 30–90 cm |
| **Family:** poppy |
| **Flowering months:** June–September |

Yellow-horned poppies grow on the shingle beds at the back of beaches. It is a strong plant that can survive coastal winds. Its leaves and stems are bluish-green and covered in rough hairs. The leaves at the base of the plant are deeply lobed. The upper leaves have shallow lobes and clasp the stem.

▼ *The yellow-horned poppy has bright yellow flowers.*

# Sea holly

**Scientific name:** *Eryngium maritimum*

**Height:** 30–60 cm

**Family:** carrot

**Flowering months:** June–September

Sea holly grows on sand and shingle. It gets its name because it has prickly leaves. The pale blue-green leaves have 3–5 lobes with white, spiny, toothed edges. It has tiny blue flowers. These are arranged in a rounded flower head, surrounded by spiny, leaf-like bracts.

▼ *Sea holly has a pale-blue colour which makes it easy to recognize.*

# Thrift

**Scientific name:** *Armeria maritima*

**Height:** 5–30 cm     **Family:** thrift

**Flowering months:** April–August

Thrift grows in clumps on rocky shores and cliffs. It also grows in grassland near to the sea. Thrift has narrow, grass-like leaves that feel slightly fleshy. The flower stems grow taller than the leaves. It has clusters of pink flowers.

◀ *Thrift needs plenty of light to grow. Its roots grow deep into splits in the rocks.*

# Moorland flowers

In Britain there are moors on the uplands and lowlands of Wales, Scotland, and parts of western and northern England. Moorland has high rainfall and the ground is damp. The soil is peaty with few nutrients. Under the soil are rocks such as granite or sandstone. These are difficult conditions for any plant or tree to grow. Among the most interesting of the moor's plants are sundews and butterworts. These plants take some of their nourishment from the bodies of insects that get stuck to them.

## Round-leaved sundew

Scientific name: *Drosera rotundifolia*

Height: 5–15 cm

Family: sundew

Flowering months: June–August

► *The remains of an insect can just be seen on the sticky leaf of this sundew plant.*

The round-leaved sundew has leaves arranged in a flat rosette. The yellowish-green leaves are covered with red glands. At the tip of each gland there are droplets of sticky liquid. When an insect gets stuck on these droplets the leaf folds up and traps the insect. The leaves produce a liquid that digests the insect's body. This nourishing 'soup' is then absorbed by the plant. The round-leaved sundew has flowers with six white petals.

## Common butterwort

◄ *The leaves are covered in sticky slime. Insects get caught in this and are then absorbed or 'eaten' by the plant.*

Scientific name: *Pinguicula vulgaris*

Height: 5–15 cm

Family: bladderwort

Flowering months: May–July

Common Butterwort grows on wet rocks and in damp soil. It has a flat rosette of yellowish-green leaves at its base. The flower stem bears a single violet flower. The flower has a two-lobed upper lip and a three-lobed lower lip. A short spur points backwards.

# Common cotton grass

**Scientific name:** *Eriophorum angustifolium*

**Height:** 20–60 cm

**Family:** sedge

**Flowering months:** May–June

▶ *In June and July common cotton grass is covered in a mass of white cottony hairs.*

Common cotton grass is a spreading plant that grows in moorland bogs. It has long, narrow leaves that end in a three-sided point. The tiny flowers are clustered together in oval flower heads. The flower heads are arranged in a cluster at the top of a tall stem. It is difficult to spot the common cotton grass until it has flowered. Then it is covered in white, cottony seed heads that seem to dance in the breeze.

# Bog asphodel

**Scientific name:** *Narthecium ossifragum*

**Height:** 5–45 cm        **Family:** lily

**Flowering months:** July–September

From July to September the bog asphodel has pretty, bright yellow flowers. As the flowers get older their colour deepens to orange. The leaves of the bog asphodel are sword-shaped. They grow in tufts at the base of the plant. There are a few small leaves on the upright flower stem.

In the past bog asphodel flowers were used to make hair dye.

◀ *Bog asphodel has star-shaped flowers. Each flower has three petals and three sepals.*

# Be a Wild Flower Detective

How do you identify different wild flowers? It is a bit like being a detective. Every species is different and you will need to look for clues. It's best to identify a wild flower when it is in bloom. First, look for flowers that you know already. Make sure that you can recognize the sepals, petals, stamens and carpels of each flower. Once you can do this then try to identify a flower you do not know by using these clues.

## WILD FLOWER DIARY

To make a wild flower diary, you will need:

- a notebook
- a camera or coloured pencils

Each month, look at the wild flowers that grow near you. Find different places to look, for example garden lawns, hedgerows, patches of wasteland and beside water.

Count how many different kinds of flowers you can see in each place. Look at the sepals, petals, stamens and carpels of each flower. Then look the flowers up in a book about wild flowers.

Now you are ready to begin writing your diary. For each entry, write down the date, the place and the different wild flowers that you found. Take a photograph or draw a picture of each flower. Label each picture with a caption.

Keep watching the wild flowers as they grow. Draw their seeds, fruits and leaves.

▲ *By keeping a wild flower diary, you will discover which flowers grow best in different places.*

◀◀▶ *White clover (left) has clusters of white flowers. Ragged robin (below) has ragged shaped petals. Common poppies (right) have large, flimsy bright red petals.*

# Protecting Wild Flowers

In recent years, some wild flowers have become rare or extinct. This is because their habitats have been changed or destroyed. New houses, roads or industrial sites have been built in the countryside. Modern farming practices have reduced other wild flower habitats. Also, the use of weedkillers has killed off many farmland wild flowers.

Wildflowers can be protected in many different ways. It is illegal for anyone to dig up a wild plant without permission from the person who owns the land. It is also illegal to pick many kinds of orchids but you can pick other common wild flowers.

Farmers play a big part in protecting wild flowers. These days some farmers don't grow crops at the side of their fields. They don't use weedkiller in these areas either. Poppies, corn marigolds and other pretty farmland weeds are left to grow. Many other wild flowers are protected because they are growing in nature reserves.

▲ *Fritillary was once a common wild flower. It grew in wet meadows in southern Britain. The meadows were drained for farming and the plants became very rare.*

◀ *The use of weedkillers by farmers has probably caused some wild flowers to disappear from the countryside forever.*

# Plant a Wild Flower Garden

You can grow your own wild flowers wherever you live. You don't even need a garden. All you need are packets of wild flower seeds. Your local garden centre should sell a good selection.

## YOU WILL NEED:

- small spade or trowel
- packets of wild flower seeds
- a small watering can

For an indoor flower garden, you will also need:

- flower pots or a small window box
- seed compost
- old newspapers

## OUTDOOR WILD FLOWER GARDEN

First you should ask your parents where you can have your garden. Then, dig the soil until it is fine and crumbly. Remove large stones and grass.

You will probably have some wild flowers growing in your garden already. Your parents might call them weeds and dig them up. Dig up some of these flowers carefully. Replant them in your garden and water them well. Now you are ready to plant the seeds.

## INDOOR WILD FLOWER GARDEN

You can make an indoor wild flower garden. Begin by spreading newspaper over a table. Place your pots on top and fill with seed compost. Now you are ready to plant the seeds.

## PLANTING THE SEEDS

On the back of the seed packet you will find instructions about how to plant your seeds. Read these instructions carefully. Different kinds of seeds need to be treated differently. Plant the seeds and water them well. Remember to water them every day.

Some seedlings may appear after a few days. Others take a few weeks. When the seedlings have at least four leaves they need to be thinned out. Dig them up gently and re-plant them further apart.

Enjoy the flowers as they come into bloom. Watch and see the different insects that visit the flowers. You could save some of the seeds from your flowers and plant them again the next year.

◀ *Read the instructions about how to plant your seeds. Some seeds might need to be lightly covered with soil. Others might need to be planted more deeply.*

▶ *This garden has some beautiful wild flowers. There are poppies, wild pansies, daisies and wild campion.*

# Glossary

**Botanists** People who study plants.

**Bracts** Leaf-like structures often found just below a flower head.

**Carpel** The female organs of a flower.

**Catkins** Short, dangling stems bearing many tiny flowers.

**Corolla** Whorls of petals that form the inner part of the flower.

**Cultivated** A plant that is grown for a particular purpose.

**Dispersed** To be scattered or spread out.

**Fertile** Soil that is rich in plant nutrients.

**Fertilization** To provide a plant with pollen about the creation of new plants.

**Florets** The many tiny flowerlets that make up the flower head of plants of the daisy family.

**Fuse** To join together.

**Germinate** When a seed swells and starts to grow.

**Glands** Tiny organs that produce, or ooze out, liquids.

**Lobe** A rounded part of a leaf or petal that hangs or sticks out.

**Nectar** A sugary substance made by flowers to attract insects that will pollinate the flower.

**Nutlets** Small, hard, nutlike seeds or fruits.

**Ovary** The female reproductive organ of a flower.

**Photosynthesis** The process that takes place in the leaves of plants. In this process energy from sunlight turns carbon dioxide in the air and water from the ground into sugar.

**Pollen** The fine dust-like grains made by the male part of the flower.

**Pollination** To transfer pollen from one flower to another in order to fertilize the plant.

**Ray florets** The florets, each with a single narrow petal, around the outer part of a flower such as a daisy.

**Ribs** Veins of a leaf.

**Rosette** A flat circle of leaves growing out from a central root.

**Sepals** The parts of a flower that protect it when it is in bud.

**Spur** A short, slender shoot.

**Stamen** The male fertilizing organ of a flower.

**Stigma** The part of the flower that receives the pollen during pollination.

**Style** The part of the flower that supports the stigma.

**Suckers** Shoots that grow up from the roots around the base of a plant.

**Whorls** Rings of leaves around the stem of a plant.

# Further information

## Books to read

*British Wild Flowers* by Brian Vesey-Fitzgerald, Rowland Hilder, Edith Hilder (Ladybird Books, 1957)

*Collins How to Identify Wild Flowers* by Christopher Grey-Wilson and Lisa Alderson (Harper Collins, 2000)

*Cycles in Nature: Plant Life* by Theresa Greenaway (Hodder Wayland, 2000)

*Eyewitness Handbooks: Wild Flowers of Britain and Northwest Europe* by Christopher Grey-Wilson (Dorling Kindersley, 1995)

*Plants: British Trees, British Plants, How Plants Grow* by Angela Royston (Heinemann, 1999)

*Pocket Guide to Wildlife of Britain and Europe* by Jeanette Harris (Kingfisher, 1988)

*Pocket Nature: Wild Flowers* by Neil Fletcher (Dorling Kindersley, 2004)

*The Earth Strikes Back: Plant Life* by Pamela Grant (Belitha, 1999)

*The Wild Flowers of Britain and Ireland* by Marjorie Blamey, Richard and Alastair Fitter (A & C Black, 2001)

*Usborne New Spotter's Guides: Wild Flowers* by C. J. Humphries (Usborne, 2000)

*Wild Flowers of the British Isles* by David Streeter (Midsummer Books, 1998)

## Websites

The Wildlife Trust: www.wildlifetrusts.org.uk

Plantlife International: www.plantlife.org.uk

Friends of the Earth: www.foe.co.uk

National Trust: www.nationaltrust.org.uk

Royal Botanical Gardens, Kew: www.rbgkew.org.uk

## Organizations to contact

Most counties in Britain have their own Wildlife Trust. Each trust arranges special visits to its reserves to look at the wild flowers, and sometimes holds courses to help people identify them. Contact the address below or look on their website to find out the address of your local Wildlife Trust.

The Wildlife Trust, The Kiln, Waterside, Mather Road,
Newark NG24 1WT
Tel: 0870 0367711

Plantlife International (a wild plant conservation charity)
14 Rollestone Street, Salisbury SP1 1DX
Tel: 01722 342730

# Index

Page numbers in **bold**
indicate pictures.